**HEINEMANN
STATE STUDIES**

# Illinois
## History

Andrew Santella

Designed by Heinemann Library
Page layout by Depke Design
Printed and bound in the United States by Lake
Book Manufacturing, Inc.

07 06 05 04 03
10 9 8 7 6 5 4 3 2 1

**Library of Congress
Cataloging-in-Publication Data**
Santella, Andrew.
  Illinois history / by Andrew Santella.
    v. cm. -- (State studies)
Includes bibliographical references and index.
Contents: Early Illinois -- Statehood -- A changing
nation -- Into the twentieth century -- A new mil-
lennium.
  ISBN 1-40340-008-3 (HC), 1-40340-569-7 (Pbk)
  1. Illinois--History--Juvenile literature. [1. Illinois--
History.] I. Title. II. State studies (Heinemann
Library (Firm))
  F541.3 .S265 2002
  977.3--dc21
                                    2002000796

**Acknowledgments**
The author and publishers are grateful to the
following for permission to reproduce copyright
material:

Cover photographs by (TL-TR): Illinois State
Historical Library; Illinois State Historical Library;
Chicago Historical Society; Photri; (bottom) Corbis

p. 4 Melissa Winter/Peabody Energy; pp. 5, 12,
16, 18, 29 maps.com/Heinemann Library;
p. 6 Jonathan Blair/Corbis; p. 7 Carter Sisney
Photography; p. 8 Courtesy of Cahokia Mounds
State Historic Site; p. 9 "Man Who Tracks, a Chief",
by George Catlin. Gift of Mrs. Joseph Harrison, Jr.,
Smithsonian American Art Museum, Washington,
D.C./Art Resource; p. 10T Michele Moldenhauer,
Archeological Society of Virginia Artist, and the
Virginia Department of Historic Resources; p. 10B,
17T, 20, 35, 40B, 44T Robert Lifson/Heinemann
Library; pp. 11, 13, 14B, 19B North Wind Pictures;
p. 14T Steve Warble; p. 15 The Granger
Collection, NY; p. 17B Francis Marion Pebbles
(1839-1928)/Chicago Historical Society; p. 19T
Henry Lewis/Wisconsin Historical Society; p. 21L
Courtesy of John Deere; pp. 21R, 22, 25, 31B
Chicago Historical Society; p. 22T Photri; p. 22B
Stock Montage; pp. 23T, 24, 26T, 27, 34, 36
Bettmann/Corbis; p. 23B Marshall Prescott/Unicorn
Stock Photos; pp. 26B, 30T, 31T, 32, 37T, 39B,
42T Corbis; p. 28 Illinois Department of
Commerce and Community Affairs; p. 30B 1898
cover: Reprinted by permission of Sears, Roebuck
and Co. Protected by copyright. No duplication
permitted; p. 33 Stock Montage; p. 38 AP/Wide
World Photos; pp. 39T, 44B Courtesy of Fermilab;
p. 40T Sandy Felsenthal/Corbis; p. 41 U.S. Senate
Historical Office; p. 42B Courtesy Ronald Reagan
Library

Every effort has been made to contact copyright
holders of any material reproduced in this book.
Any omissions will be rectified in subsequent
printings if notice is given to the publisher.

Some words are shown in bold, **like this.**
You can find out what they mean by looking
in the glossary.

# Contents

# Early Illinois

**L**ong before people lived in Illinois, natural forces were shaping it. Millions of years ago, a watery swamp covered Illinois. Eventually, the trees and plants of the swamp died. They sank under water and formed a kind of spongy soil called **peat.** Over many years, the weight of layers of rock and sand hardened the peat. Eventually, it turned into a black rock that we call **bituminous coal.** Today, people dig coal from the ground and burn it for heat and energy. Illinois sits atop the nation's largest supply of bituminous coal.

Long after the swamps dried up, huge glaciers stretched over Illinois. Glaciers are thick sheets of ice that do not melt as the seasons change. They can slowly spread over land, and just as slowly melt and retreat. Thousands of years ago, glaciers inched their

*Illinois coal mines provide over 40 million tons (36 million metric tons) of coal each year.*

4

**Illinois**

- Galena
- Rockford
- Byron
- Elgin
- Waukegan
- Arlington Heights
- Des Plaines
- Evanston
- Skokie
- Oak Park
- Chicago
- Dixon
- Wheaton
- Aurora
- Naperville
- Joliet
- *Illinois & Michigan Canal*
- Rock Island
- Moline
- Tampico
- La Salle
- Kankakee
- Bishop Hill
- Galesburg
- *Illinois River*
- Peoria
- Eureka
- Pekin
- Normal
- Bloomington
- Nauvoo
- Champaign
- Danville
- Urbana
- *Sangamon River*
- Quincy
- New Salem
- Springfield
- Arthur
- *Lake Shelbyville*
- Mattoon
- *Illinois River*
- *Kaskaskia River*
- Effingham
- *Embarras River*
- Godfrey
- Vandalia
- Alton
- Edwardsville
- *Carlyle Lake*
- East St. Louis
- Cahokia
- Centralia
- *Wabash River*
- Mt. Vernon
- Grayville
- Prairie du Rocher
- *Rend Lake*
- Kaskaskia
- *Big Muddy River*
- Shawneetown
- *Mississippi River*
- Carbondale
- *Ohio River*
- Cairo
- *Fox River*
- *Rock River*
- *Kankakee River*

N W E S

| 0 | 50 mi. |
| 0 | 50 km |

way down from the north to cover Illinois. Four times the
glaciers advanced, and four times they retreated. Each
advance and retreat took tens of thousands of years.

The glaciers helped shape the way Illinois looks today.
They were so heavy that they flattened the land. They
dug into the earth to create lake beds and river chan-
nels. When the glaciers melted about 15,000 years ago,
the force of rushing water cut into hard rock to form
beautiful cliffs. When the glaciers inched away, they left

*The woolly mammoth (right) is an extinct relative of the modern elephant. Some mammoths were more than 14 feet (4.3 meters) tall, with tusks 13 feet (4 meters) long. Their long hair helped protect them from the severe cold of the **Ice Age.***

*Farms are found in every part of Illinois. The rich prairie soil is perfect for farming (below, background).*

behind finely ground bits of rock. Those bits of rock were full of the minerals that make soil rich. Thousands of kinds of grasses and other plants grew in that rich soil. Much of Illinois was covered with **prairie** up through the 1700s. In the 1800s, farms began to take the place of the prairie. Today, that same rich soil helps make Illinois one of the nation's leading farm states.

## THE FIRST ILLINOISANS

The first people to live in Illinois arrived about 15,000 years ago. They were wandering hunters, or **nomads.** They followed the herds of wild animals they depended on for food. These early residents of the Americas were descended from **Stone Age** people. The Stone Age people had originally come from Asia to North America across the **Bering Strait.** Over many years, groups of people moved south from what are now Alaska and Canada to settle all across North and South America.

The first Illinoisans did not live in permanent, or fixed, settlements. They made camps in forests to be near the animals they hunted. Many of the large animals they hunted are now **extinct** (no longer living), like the **woolly mammoth** and the **mastodon.** These early Illinoisans are called Paleo-Indians, which means

*Here is an atlatl in use. A spear launched with an atlatl could travel faster and farther than one thrown by hand. This helped people hunt large animals like the mammoth.*

"ancient Indians." They hunted on foot because there were no horses in America at that time. They wrapped themselves in animal skins to keep warm in a climate that was much colder than today's.

About 5,000 years ago, the Indians of the **Archaic Period** began planting crops and harvesting them. These people were Illinois's first farmers. They also gathered fruits and nuts. The people of the Archaic Period invented new tools for hunting. One of the tools was called an atlatl. An atlatl was a wooden tool used for launching spears. A spear launched with an atlatl could travel a greater distance than one thrown by hand. This helped make people of the Archaic Period better hunters.

People of the Woodland Culture in Illinois were the first to build villages and burial mounds. The Woodland Culture lasted from about 1000 B.C.E. to about C.E. 700. Woodland people invented the bow and arrow for use in hunting. They also began making pottery. These people

*Monks Mound (left) is located near the present-day city of Collinsville, Illinois. It is the largest prehistoric earthwork in the United States. Visitors can still climb the mound today.*

*This is an artist's recreation (right) of what the Mississippian city of Cahokia may have looked like in C.E. 1150. Monks Mound is visible in the distance.*

were part of a large trading network. They traded for seashells from the Gulf of Mexico and for copper mined near Lake Superior. They were the first to grow corn in Illinois. Anyone who has driven across Illinois recently knows that Illinoisans are still outstanding corn farmers. Illinois is one of the country's top corn producers.

Around the year C.E. 900, people living near the Mississippi River began building a grand city. They were part of a new culture called the Mississippian Culture. The Mississippian Period lasted from about C.E. 800 to about C.E. 1500. The Mississippian city of Cahokia held as many as 20,000 people. It spread over six square miles (fifteen square kilometers) near the present-day city of Collinsville, Illinois. At the center of the city there was a 100-foot (30-meter) mound that covered about 17 acres (7 hectares). The mound was probably used as a temple. It is called Monks Mound and it still stands today. Monks Mound is the largest **prehistoric** earthwork in North America. Nearby, there are about 100 smaller mounds that were used as burial places.

# Woodhenge

**Archaeologists** exploring near Monks Mound found a mysterious circle of holes in the ground. These holes once held a ring of wooden poles made of cedar. People of the Mississippian Culture used the poles to measure the sun's position in the sky and keep track of time. The circle of poles may have been used as a place for religious rituals. The site reminded some people of England's Stonehenge, so they named it Woodhenge.

The people of the Mississippian Culture probably practiced astronomy, which is the study of the stars. They performed **sacred rituals** in large **plazas.** But by 1500, the people abandoned their cities and temples. No one is sure exactly what happened. However, by the time the first Europeans arrived in Illinois, the cities were empty.

## NATIVE AMERICANS IN ILLINOIS

Not long after the decline of the Mississippian Culture around 1500, a new group of people came to the area. The new people would give their name to the land they called home. They were the Native Americans of the Illinois Nation, also known as the Illinois **Confederacy.** The Illinois Nation was a group of tribes that shared a common language and defended each other against common enemies. The tribes included the Peoria, Kaskaskia, Tamaroa, Cahokia, Moingwena, and Michigamea, among others. They called themselves *Illiniwek,* which roughly translated is, "the men." They all spoke Algonquin, a language shared by many Native American nations of eastern North America.

*This is an 1830 painting of Pah-me-cow-e-tah (Man Who Tracks), a Peoria chief. The Peoria were part of the Illinois Confederacy.*

*The Illinois tribes lived in longhouses (left) in the summer, and wigwams (right) in the winter. Both types of house were made of wood poles covered with layers of woven mats. Longhouses were divided into rooms, with a fire pit for each family.*

The Illinois tribes lived in what are now Wisconsin and Iowa, and in parts of Missouri and Arkansas, in addition to Illinois. They built their villages along major rivers. In the summer, they lived in large, rectangular houses called longhouses. Longhouses were usually shared by six to ten families. The longhouses were located in the larger, more permanent villages, where the Illinois tribes farmed. In the winter, the Illinois split into smaller groups for hunting and set up smaller villages. Their winter villages had dome-shaped houses called **wigwams.** Wigwams were smaller and could be moved more easily. The Illinois grew corn and other crops. They also hunted **bison.** The Illinois worshipped a supreme being called the Master of Life. They also believed in spirits called *manitous,* which could take the form of animals or birds.

The Illinois were not the only Native Americans who lived in the state named for them. The Miami lived in northern Illinois, near Lake Michigan. Around 1650, Iroquois people began invading Illinois. The Iroquois were among the most

## Starved Rock

Starved Rock (right) is a 130-foot (40-meter) cliff that towers over the Illinois River. According to legend,

a group of Illinois was trapped atop the rock by the attack of a neighboring tribe. The Illinois were surrounded, and many starved to death there.

feared of Native American nations. They traded with English and Dutch settlers in New York for guns. They sometimes used those guns to fight other tribes. The Iroquois knew Illinois had many beavers. Beaver **pelts** were valuable trade items. Iroquois war parties began attacking the Illinois people. In the late 1600s, other tribes moved into Illinois as well. These included the Sauk, Fox, Winnebago, Potawatomi, Kickapoo, and Shawnee.

## FRENCH EXPLORERS

Around the same time, another group of people came to Illinois territory. One day in 1673, two men walked into an Illinois tribal village near present-day Keokuk, Iowa. The two men were unlike any the Illinois had seen before. Their names were Father Jacques Marquette and Louis Jolliet. They were probably the first Frenchmen the Illinois had ever met.

Marquette and Jolliet were in the middle of a long journey down the Mississippi River. Their goals were to convert

*After his trip through Illinois, Marquette wrote an account of the voyage. His journals help historians form a clearer picture of early French activities in the Illinois region.*

# French Exploration

Jolliet and Marquette, 1673

Sieur de La Salle, 1681–1682

Present-day state of Illinois

Mounds

Native Village

Fort

*French explorers found the rivers of Illinois as valuable for transportation as the native peoples had for hundreds of years.*

Native Americans they met to **Christianity** and extend France's empire in North America. They wanted to use the Mississippi River as a highway to carry furs from the middle of North America to the Great Lakes. From there, they could reach French settlements in Canada and eventually make their way to Europe. Marquette and Jolliet quickly made friends with the Illinois people. The Native Americans told the explorers about a shortcut through Illinois country. Marquette and Jolliet followed the shortcut on their return trip. It took them past the place where Chicago would one day rise.

Another French explorer, René-Robert Cavelier, Sieur de La Salle, built a **fort** along the route Marquette and Jolliet had followed. It was located near present-day Peoria. People of the Illinois Nation gathered there to trade with the French. They also looked to the French for protection. Like the Illinois, the French considered the Iroquois a threat. La Salle became friends with the Illinois and promised to protect them.

Over the next 100 years, the French built forts and cities along the rivers of Illinois. The towns of Kaskaskia and

Cahokia, in southern Illinois, were started as French trading posts or **missions.** They were to be part of a string of French **strongholds** along the Mississippi and Illinois Rivers.

The French dream of an empire did not last. France was defeated in the **French and Indian War** with Great Britain, which took place from 1754 to 1763. France had to give up its North American possessions. In 1765, British troops raised the British flag over Illinois.

## Life in French Illinois

Most French villages in Illinois grew up around **Catholic** missions. Religion was the center of village life. French priests taught the children of the village and led daily religious services. The French celebrated 27 religious holidays each year. Most of the villagers were named for saints. Each person celebrated his or her saint's feast day once a year, instead of his or her own birthday.

The French lived in houses made of logs stuck upright in the ground. The gaps between logs were filled with a mixture of clay and grass. A wooden porch often extended all the way around the house.

French villages included not only French people, but also Native Americans and African slaves. In 1720, the first African slaves were brought to Illinois to work on French farms. The French required slaveholders to educate their slaves and **baptize** them in the Catholic religion. Slaves lived in separate houses near their owner's house. Native Americans traded with French villagers and sometimes took religion lessons from French priests. French men outnumbered French women in Illinois. Some French men married Native American women.

Children in the French villages were expected to grow up quickly. When a boy turned twelve, he was considered old enough to carry a gun and defend the settlement. When a girl turned twelve, she was considered old enough to marry.

## Liberty Bell of the West

After George Rogers Clark captured Kaskaskia, the townspeople rang the village church bell in celebration. The date was July 4, 1778—the second anniversary of the signing of the Declaration of Independence. The bell (right) became known as the Liberty Bell of the West.

### THE AMERICAN REVOLUTION

The British had little interest in Illinois because it was far from their colonies along the Atlantic Ocean. When those colonies declared their independence in 1776, the British had very few troops in Illinois. Most of the fighting in the American Revolutionary War (1775–1783) happened far to the east. However, one important campaign brought the Revolution to Illinois.

*George Rogers Clark (below) left Kentucky in 1778 to take Kaskaskia from the British. He then led a small force across rough winter terrain to capture Vincennes, Indiana.*

In 1778, a Virginian named George Rogers Clark led 175 volunteers to capture British **forts** in Illinois. Striking quickly and by surprise, Clark's troops captured Kaskaskia and surrounding towns in southern Illinois. Then Clark led his men on a daring attack on British troops at Vincennes, in what is now Indiana. His victory there meant that Illinois would one day become part of the United States.

# Statehood

**A**fter the American victory in the Revolutionary War, Illinois became part of the new United States. Lands west of the Appalachian Mountains were first organized as **territories.** As the population grew, an area could apply to Congress to become a state.

In 1787, the United States government created the Northwest Territory. It included the land between the Great Lakes and Ohio River. Parts of this land would become Ohio, Indiana, Michigan, Wisconsin, Illinois, and part of Minnesota.

## SETTLING ILLINOIS

When the Northwest Territory was formed, the land that would become Illinois was thinly settled. In 1800, only about 2,500 people lived in Illinois. However, twelve thousand new settlers entered Illinois in the next ten years. In 1809, the U.S. Congress made Illinois a separate territory. Kaskaskia became the first territorial capital.

At around the same time, a settlement was appearing on the shores of Lake Michigan. It was started by Jean-Baptiste Point Du Sable, a trader

*This is what Chicago and Fort Dearborn probably looked like around 1820. With Lake Michigan and nearby rivers, this location was very valuable for trade.*

## Illinois and the Northwest Territory

The Northwest Territory was created in 1787. Many new territories, and eventually states, came out of the Northwest Territory.

from Haiti. His trading post grew, and the area became more important as people moved west. In 1803, **Fort Dearborn** was constructed to protect the area. This settlement would one day grow into the city of Chicago.

Many of the people moving to Illinois traveled by riverboat. This was faster and easier than traveling by land. In 1811, the first steamboat traveled down the Ohio River, opening the way for more settlers. The new settlers built towns in southern Illinois, along the Ohio, Wabash, and Mississippi Rivers. Many settlers came from Kentucky and Tennessee.

In 1812, war broke out again between the United States and Great Britain. British commanders in Canada encouraged tribes of the Great Lakes region to attack frontier settlements. On August

## Illinois Earthquake

On December 17, 1811, the residents of the Illinois Territory received a shock. An earthquake on the New Madrid **fault** shook Illinois and the rest of the Midwest. The force of the earthquake was so strong that the course of the Mississippi River changed in several places. A large earthquake like this could happen again, but scientists think they only happen every 500–1,000 years on this fault.

15, 1812, Potawatomi warriors attacked soldiers and civilians who were fleeing Fort Dearborn. They killed about 75 people and burned the fort to the ground. This war, called the War of 1812, lasted until 1814, when the United States and Great Britain signed a peace treaty in Belgium.

*This plaque stands in Chicago in memory of Fort Dearborn and the loss of life that occurred there in 1812.*

## BECOMING A STATE

The tragedy at Fort Dearborn discouraged some settlers, but it didn't stop Illinois's growth. By 1818, over 34,000 people lived in Illinois. On December 3, 1818, Illinois became the twenty-first state in the Union. The state government rented a brick building in Kaskaskia for four dollars per day and used it as the state capitol.

Illinois gained statehood largely because of the efforts of Nathaniel Pope. Pope was Illinois's representative to the U.S. Congress. He worked with his nephew, Daniel Pope Cook, to build support for statehood. Pope also drew the map of the new state.

*If not for Nathaniel Pope (below), most of northern Illinois would now be part of Wisconsin.*

At first, Illinois's northern border was to be just south of Lake Michigan. However, Pope recognized that the Lake Michigan shoreline would be a great advantage for a new state. Ports on the lake would help encourage trade and attract new settlers. It would also link Illinois

17

# Moving Capitals

Kaskaskia was Illinois's state capital for just two years. In 1820, Illinois moved its capital to Vandalia. Vandalia was a new city built to house the state government. It served as the capital through 1837. That year, voters decided the capital should be located closer to the center of the state. They voted to move the state government to Springfield, where it remains today.

to the other Great Lakes, which stretched all the way to the eastern United States. Pope persuaded Congress to move the northern border of Illinois 40 miles (64 kilometers) north. If not for his efforts, most of northern Illinois would be part of Wisconsin today.

*The St. Lawrence Seaway opened over 100 years after the Erie Canal, in 1959. About 50 million tons (45 million metric tons) of freight are transported on it each year.*

## Important Waterways

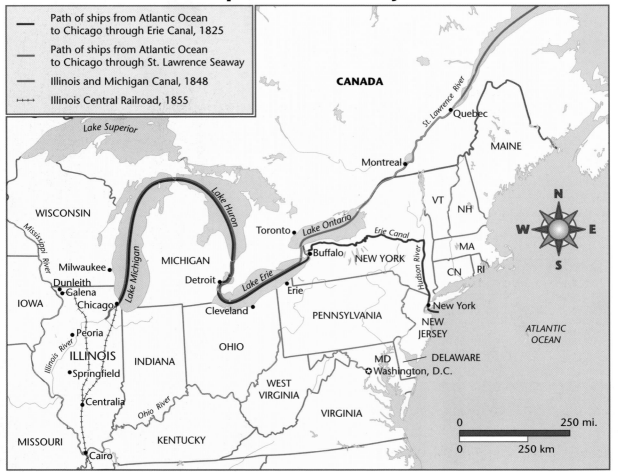

Path of ships from Atlantic Ocean to Chicago through Erie Canal, 1825

Path of ships from Atlantic Ocean to Chicago through St. Lawrence Seaway

Illinois and Michigan Canal, 1848

Illinois Central Railroad, 1855

*This illustration shows the Battle of Bad Axe at the end of the Black Hawk War (1832). Many of Black Hawk's people were killed as they tried to cross the Mississippi River to safety.*

The new state was ideally located to receive new settlers. Settlers from the south could get to Illinois by using the Ohio and Mississippi Rivers. In the north, large boats could travel to Illinois through Lake Michigan. The opening of the Erie Canal in New York in 1825 made it possible for steamboats to travel all the way from the Hudson River to Lake Michigan. Thousands of people from New York and New England traveled west over the next few decades.

These settlers demanded more and more land. This spelled doom for the Native Americans remaining in Illinois. As more white settlers moved into the state, they forced the Native Americans out. Most Illinois tribes moved west across the Mississippi River. The remaining Native Americans made their last stand in Illinois in 1832. That year, a chief named Black Hawk led about 1,000 Sauk and Fox people into the Rock River area of northwest Illinois. They wanted to plant crops there, as they had for centuries. However, the U.S. government sent troops to force Black Hawk and his people to move off the land. U.S. Army soldiers and Illinois volunteers chased Black Hawk's people into present-day Wisconsin. Many of Black

*Black Hawk (right) was a Sauk war chief. He took his name from the sparrow hawk, his guardian spirit.*

Hawk's people were killed in the Battle of Bad Axe, as they tried to cross the Mississippi River into Iowa. The Black Hawk War ended 150 years of conflict between Native Americans and white settlers in Illinois.

## WORKING THE LAND

Settlers moved in to work the land Native Americans had once farmed. Much of central Illinois was covered by level grasslands called **prairies.** The flat land stretched as far as the eye could see, covered by nothing but tall grass and wildflowers. Those flowers and grasses could be beautiful, but they caused trouble for farmers. Prairie plants send roots deep into the soil. Some roots might extend 15 feet (4.5 meters) beneath the surface. Farmers had difficulty cutting through the tough roots. Preparing a field for planting could be backbreaking labor.

To help solve these problems, an Illinois **blacksmith** named John Deere invented a new plow in 1838. Deere's plow was made of polished steel instead of cast iron, so it sliced cleanly through the thickest roots. The steel of the

*The first settlers avoided the prairies of Illinois. But Deere's plow allowed farmers to cut cleanly through the tough roots of prairie grasses and successfully farm the whole state.*

# Life on the Farm

Early Illinois farmers faced many hardships. Many lived on lonely homesteads far from their nearest neighbors. Bad weather, sudden fires started by lightning, and diseases like **malaria** made life difficult. Only determination and hard work helped Illinois farmers make it through hard times.

Farm children were expected to do their share of the work. Farm animals had to be fed and cared for. Worn clothes and shoes had to be repaired. Without modern plumbing, even getting a drink of water was hard work. Water had to be pumped from a well, then lugged back to the house in heavy buckets. The most intense work happened during spring planting and the fall harvest. During these times, the family might work from sunrise to sundown. Children often had to miss school to help out with the farm work. In fact, many farm children only went to school some of the time. Some dropped out after a year or two. Others didn't start school until they were in their teens. Instead, they depended on their parents or older brothers and sisters to teach them to read and write.

plow was so smooth that soil slid right off. Deere's plow helped farmers clear the land and plant more crops.

Cyrus McCormick's invention of the reaper also helped farmers. A reaper is a machine that helps harvest grain. McCormick made the first reaper in 1831. He then began selling them in Illinois and neighboring states.

*In 1838, John Deere (right) invented a steel plow (left) that could cut through the tough roots of prairie grasses without the dirt sticking. This allowed settlers to farm the entire state of Illinois.*

*Cyrus McCormick (below, right) made his first reaper (top, right) in 1831. The reaper allowed farmers to harvest larger amounts of grain more quickly. McCormick sold his reapers all over the United States.*

In 1847, he opened a factory in Chicago to produce reapers. It was the largest factory in Chicago at that time.

### RAILROADS AND CANALS

In 1836, the state began building a canal that would link Lake Michigan and the Illinois River. The Illinois and Michigan Canal (see map on page 18) made it possible for boats to travel through the Great Lakes, to the Mississippi River, and down to the Gulf of Mexico. It helped speed up the growth of Chicago and Illinois businesses.

Not long after the canal was completed in 1848, Illinois's first railroad began operation. The Illinois Central Railroad (see map on page 18) ran from Cairo, at Illinois's southern tip, to Dunleith, in the northwest corner of the state. The first trains ran in 1855. At the time, the Illinois Central was the longest railroad in the world.

### SLAVERY

As Illinois grew, it became divided over the issue of slavery. Since the French began settling in Illinois, people in the state had owned slaves. The Northwest Ordinance of 1787 made it illegal to bring new slaves into the territory. However, it did not free slaves already in the territory. Not until 1848, with the passage of a new state constitution, was slavery finally abolished in Illinois.

*A mob murdered Elijah Lovejoy in 1837 because he had spoken out against slavery.*

22

Many Illinoisans came from southern states and had grown up with slavery. Others were **abolitionists.** Abolitionists were people who believed slavery was wrong and should be outlawed everywhere. An abolitionist in Alton, Illinois, named Elijah P. Lovejoy wrote newspaper articles speaking out against slavery. Angry mobs of slavery supporters destroyed his printing presses again and again. On November 7, 1837, a mob murdered Lovejoy.

Some Illinoisans fought slavery by helping slaves escape. They helped slaves flee on the **Underground Railroad.** This was not an actual railroad, nor was it under the ground. It was a route slaves followed to freedom in the North or in Canada. Escaped slaves could stop at certain locations, where they would be hidden by abolitionists.

In 1857, the argument over slavery reached the U.S. Supreme Court. The historic court case involved a slave living in Illinois named Dred Scott. Scott's owner had moved to Illinois from Missouri. In Missouri, slavery was legal. In this famous 1857 case, the U.S. Supreme Court ruled that Scott remained a slave even when he left Missouri and moved into Illinois. The court also ruled that slaves were property and could not be citizens or hold any rights. The ruling angered opponents of slavery.

*Dred Scott (above) was sold shortly after his famous court case. His new owner freed him, two months after the court decision.*

# The Underground Railroad

Dozens of Illinois churches, homes, and shops have been identified as Underground Railroad stops. One of the people who helped escaped slaves on the Underground Railroad was Elijah Lovejoy's brother, Owen. He hid escaped slaves in a secret space in his attic. Owen Lovejoy's house (left) still exists today. It is located in Princeton, Illinois.

In 1858, the argument over slavery affected the election for the U.S. Senate in Illinois. That year, a young lawyer named Abraham Lincoln ran against Stephen A. Douglas.

Lincoln believed slavery should not be allowed to spread to new states. Douglas believed new states should decide for themselves whether or not they wanted slavery. The two men debated seven times during the election campaign. Reports of the debates were printed in newspapers all over the country. They helped make Lincoln a national star. However, they did not help him win the 1858 election. Douglas became the next senator from Illinois.

Even though he lost, Lincoln's words had impressed voters. People remembered his words two years later, when he ran for president. One of his opponents in the 1860 election was Douglas. It was the first time two men from the same state competed for president. This time, Lincoln won.

*When Lincoln entered the Senate race, he said, "a house divided against itself cannot stand. I believe that this government cannot endure permanently half slave and half free." Slavery was the main issue in 1858, and would be the main issue throughout Lincoln's political life.*

# A Changing Nation

**A**s president, Lincoln wanted to unite the country. But his election angered many southerners. They feared he would try to put an end to slavery in the South. Many southerners had vowed that their states would leave the Union if voters elected Lincoln. When Lincoln won the election, seven southern states left the Union. On April 12, 1861, **rebels** fired on **Fort** Sumter in South Carolina. The Civil War had begun.

Lincoln's leadership helped hold the country together during the Civil War (1861–1865). Many people in Washington, D.C., made fun of Lincoln's country ways. They poked fun at his appearance and unfashionable clothes. Lincoln had little experience as a public official, and some people wondered if he could succeed as president during a time of crisis. Lincoln proved ready for the job. His words and actions guided the American people through the crisis. In 1863, Lincoln made a speech at the dedication of a cemetery near a battlefield in Gettysburg, Pennsylvania. The speech became known as the Gettysburg Address. It explained to Americans why it was important to hold the Union together. In another speech at his second **inauguration** in 1865, he urged the North to welcome the South back into the Union after the war.

*Abraham Lincoln was determined to hold the Union together. He brought the United States through its worst crisis.*

*A special funeral train (right) carried President Lincoln's body back to Springfield. Thousands of people came to pay their respects as the train passed through their towns.*

Most importantly, Lincoln led the nation toward abolishing slavery. In 1863, he issued the Emancipation Proclamation. It freed all the slaves living in the southern states that had left the Union. It was the first step toward ending the injustice of slavery. Slavery was finally outlawed in 1865 with the Thirteenth Amendment to the U.S. Constitution. Lincoln never saw his nation reunited. On April 14, 1865, President Lincoln and his wife, Mary, attended a play called *Our American Cousin* at Ford's Theater in Washington, D.C. A man named John Wilkes Booth shot the president while he watched the play. Lincoln died the next morning. His body was returned to Springfield, Illinois, by a special funeral train. Thousands of Americans lined the railroad tracks across the nation to watch the train pass. Lincoln was buried in Springfield on May 4, 1865.

## THE CIVIL WAR

Lincoln was one of many Illinoisans who gave his life for his country during the Civil War (1861–1865). Illinois sent 259,092 men to fight the war. Nearly 35,000 of them died. Illinois provided 177 of the Union Army's generals. One of these generals was Ulysses S. Grant. Grant was working in his brother's store in Galena, Illinois, when the war broke out in

*Grant (below) led the Union forces to victory in the Civil War. He was later elected the eighteenth president of the U.S.*

1861. Since he had served as an officer in the army before, he enlisted in the war effort and was made a general. In 1864, Lincoln placed Grant in charge of all Union armies. In 1865, Grant finally forced the **rebel** army led by Robert E. Lee to surrender.

Grant arranged to meet Lee at Appomattox Court House in Virginia to accept his surrender. Grant brought a friend from Illinois named Ely Parker to the historic meeting. Parker was Grant's aide and a Seneca tribesman. He wrote the terms of surrender that Lee signed on April 9, 1865.

Common citizens of Illinois contributed to the war effort, too. Farmers helped feed the Union armies. Illinois women volunteered to sew uniforms and prepare bandages for hospitals. Others worked as nurses in **crude** hospitals near battlefields.

A widow from Galesburg named Mary Ann Bickerdyke saved many lives by improving hospitals. The poor conditions made it difficult for wounded men to recover. Bickerdyke worked to make hospitals cleaner and more comfortable. The Union soldiers lovingly called her "Mother Bickerdyke."

*Bickerdyke (above) worked hard to clean up Union hospitals. She didn't hesitate to confront generals to get what she needed.*

About a year after the Civil War ended, the people of one Illinois town gathered to remember their fallen soldiers. On April 29, 1866, the citizens of Carbondale met in a local cemetery for the nation's first Memorial Day. Memorial Day is now celebrated on the fourth Monday in May and has been a federal holiday since 1971.

## THE INDUSTRIAL AGE

With the war over, Illinois began a period of new growth. The state's population rose quickly. In 1868, Illinois began construction of a new capitol building in Springfield to house a growing state government. The building took twenty years to complete. It is still the home of Illinois's state government. In Champaign County, the Illinois Industrial University opened in 1867. The college later became known as the University of Illinois. Today, more than 30,000 students from all over the world attend classes there.

By the 1860s, railroads stretched across the country. Illinois was a crossroads for many railroad lines. It had more miles of track than any other state. Illinois became a center for transportation and **industry.**

New businesses and industries appeared all over the state. In 1865, the Union Stockyards opened in Chicago (see photo on page 30). They stood on more than 475 acres (192 hectares) of land on the city's South Side. Railroads shipped animals there from all over the country. At the stockyards, meat was prepared, packed, and shipped in refrigerated railroad cars to other cities. Chicago became a leading center for meat packaging. East St. Louis, Illinois, had its own stockyards, too.

*The Illinois state capitol building (left) was completed in 1888. Its dome is actually 74 feet (22.5 meters) taller than the U.S. Capitol dome.*

In 1868, the Chicago Iron Company was the first to build huge blast furnaces for making steel. Companies in Joliet, Belleville, and Edwardsville also made steel. By 1880, Illinois was fourth in the nation in steel production.

Joseph F. Glidden of DeKalb developed the barbed-wire fence in 1873. The fence kept livestock out of farm fields. It became popular all over the West. Peoria became a center for liquor manufacturing. In Murphysboro, companies turned local clay into bricks. Even early baseball equipment was made in Illinois. Starting in 1876, the Spalding Company of Chicago made bats and balls.

Illinois merchants were the first to let their customers shop by mail. In 1872, Montgomery Ward began mailing his catalog to farm families who could not travel to the city to buy goods. With his catalog, they could shop for clothes and furniture without leaving home. In 1887, Sears, Roebuck and Company introduced its own catalog. Customers could even buy a complete new house from the Sears catalog.

## Illinois: A Crossroads, 1860

**Railroads depicted in map**

| | |
|---|---|
| **1** — Chicago-Burlington-Quincy | **7** — Ohio & Mississippi |
| **2** — Chicago & Milwaukee | **8** — Peoria & Oquawka |
| **3** — Chicago & Northwestern | **9** — Rock Island |
| **4** — Galena-Chicago Line | **10** — St. Louis-Alton & Chicago |
| **5** — Illinois Central | **11** — Terre Haute & Alton |
| **6** — Illinois River RR | **12** — Toledo, Wabash & Great Western |

*Because of its location in the United States, Illinois became a center for transportation. In fact, it had more miles of railroad track than any other state in the 1860s.*

## CHICAGO'S GROWTH

Chicago grew very quickly after the Civil War. However, the city was nearly destroyed by a fire that started on

*The Chicago Union Stockyards processed 2 million animals each year by 1870. At that time, waste from the animals flowed into the Chicago River and then into Lake Michigan.*

October 8, 1871. The cause of the fire is still unknown. It started in the cow barn at the rear of Patrick O'Leary's cottage on Chicago's West Side. Most of the city's buildings at that time were made of wood and burned easily. The flames jumped from one side of the Chicago River to the other and kept burning. When the fire finally died out, the city was in ruins. About 300 people died in the fire, and 100,000 lost their homes. Many businesses were destroyed.

Chicago did survive. **Immigrants** from all over the world came to Chicago to help build new homes and businesses. **Architects** made plans for a bigger and better city. They developed new styles and building methods. The world's first **skyscrapers** were built in Chicago. **Industries** thrived, and the city kept growing. By 1900, Chicago was the second-largest city in the United States.

## HARD TIMES AND CONFLICT

Business boomed and industry grew, but common people still struggled. The 1860s and 1870s were hard times for Illinois farmers. During the Civil War (1861–1865), farmers produced huge crops of corn to feed the Union armies. After the war, there

*The Sears catalog allowed people outside of cities to shop for goods they couldn't get locally.*

30

# World-Class City

Chicago hosted a World's Fair in 1893. It was called the World's Columbian Exposition. The fair was supposed to mark the 400th anniversary of Christopher Columbus's voyage to America in 1492. It started a year late due to delays in planning. Twenty-seven million people from seventy-two countries visited the fair. It was located on grounds along Lake Michigan. People who went to the fair saw such attractions as the world's first Ferris wheel (left). The exhibit buildings were designed by some of the world's top architects. The fair showed the world how Chicago had bounced back from the Great Chicago Fire of 1871.

was more corn than people needed. As a result, farmers had to accept lower prices for their corn.

In addition, large, powerful railroads often cheated small farmers. Farmers depended on the railroads to get their crops to the market. Some railroads charged very high fees to ship crops. Farmers had no choice but to pay what the railroads demanded. Farmers began organizing in order to resist unfair treatment. In 1868, they began forming local clubs called **granges.** Granges supported politicians who would protect small farmers.

In the late 1800s, some businessmen made huge fortunes. At the same time, the lives of most workers remained difficult. Most people worked long hours in unsafe conditions for little pay. To fight for better

*This photograph was taken from the Chicago Water Tower after the Great Fire in 1871. The fire destroyed 18,000 buildings.*

*The Haymarket **Riot** (right) took place on May 4, 1886, during a time when thousands of workers across the country were occasionally on strike. It developed from a fight a day earlier between strikers and strike breakers at the McCormick Harvester plant.*

pay and safer workplaces, workers formed labor unions. Labor unions are groups of workers who try to convince their employers to improve conditions or raise pay. Labor unions and business owners sometimes became enemies. Most business owners ignored the demands of labor unions. To make owners pay attention, union members sometimes went on strike. During a strike, employees protest low pay or poor conditions by refusing to work.

Strikes often turned violent. In 1877, railroad workers in East St. Louis, Carbondale, and Peoria went on strike to protest low pay. It was called the Great Railroad Strike. In Chicago, striking workers fought with police officers and nineteen people died.

In the 1880s, employers often made workers work very long days. Workers all over the state began demanding an eight-hour work day. On May 4, 1886, about 1,500 workers gathered at Haymarket Square in Chicago in support of the eight-hour workday. Later that evening, police officers tried to make the last demonstrators leave. In the confusion, a bomb exploded in the middle of the crowd. Eight people were killed. Most people blamed labor unions for the violence. As a result, unions became very unpopular. However, the struggle to improve the lives of common people in Illinois went on.

# Into the Twentieth Century

**A**s a new century approached, more people began working for social change in Illinois. In 1889, Jane Addams began helping poor women and children in Chicago. She opened Hull House, which was a place where people in need could come for assistance. Families could find medical care there. Children attended classes. Adults could get help finding jobs. Everyone could use the library, gymnasium, and art gallery there.

Addams also worked to pass laws that would protect children. In 1883, the state passed a law that required children to attend school. In 1903, Illinois limited the number of hours children could work in factories. In 1931, Addams received the **Nobel Peace Prize** for her work. She was the first woman to win the important prize.

## FIGHTING FOR RIGHTS

In 1920, the Nineteenth Amendment to the U.S. Constitution finally gave women full voting rights. An organization called the Women's Christian Temperance Union led the campaign to give women the right to vote. The Women's Christian Temperance

*Jane Addams is pictured here with children at the Hull House. Residents of the house organized the first public playground and kindergarten in Chicago.*

# Children at Work

Employers in the 1890s and early 1900s looked for people who would work for little pay. They often turned to children. Children as young as six years old worked in the stockyards and factories of Chicago and other large cities. Their workday might last as long as fourteen hours, but they were often paid less than a dollar for a day's work. Children of poor parents had to work to help their families survive. They often lived in crowded **tenements,** with few windows and little fresh air. Some poor families shared apartments with several other families.

Union was based in Evanston, Illinois. In 1913, Illinois became the first state east of the Mississippi River to allow women to vote for president. In 1916, more than 200,000 Illinois women voted in the presidential election.

Others fought for their rights at the same time. Thousands of African Americans moved to Illinois from the South between 1910 and 1950. This became known as the Great Migration. They came looking for jobs in the many new factories. The United States entered World War I in 1917. Illinois factories expanded to produce goods for the war effort. African Americans found jobs in Illinois cities that they couldn't find in the South.

African Americans still faced injustice in the North. In East St. Louis, white workers became angry when African Americans took jobs from striking workers. Tensions between African Americans and whites led to violence in several Illinois cities. Race **riots** broke out in Springfield and in East St. Louis. In 1919, rioting broke out in Chicago. It started on July 27, when an African-American teenager swam too close to a beach where only white people were allowed. After 5 days of rioting, 38 people were dead, and many more were wounded or left homeless.

*Oscar De Priest (below) was elected to the United States Congress in 1928. His father had actually been a slave.*

To protect their rights, African Americans began electing their own leaders. In 1928, Oscar De Priest was elected as the first African-American congressman from Illinois.

## REFORMING ILLINOIS

Illinois also took steps to make the state a healthier place. For years, people in Chicago had unsafe drinking water. The Chicago River flowed into Lake Michigan. Garbage in the river polluted the drinking water in the lake. In 1900, the state completed a remarkable project to fix that problem. The Sanitary and Ship Canal opened south of Chicago. It ran 28 miles (45 kilometers) and connected the Chicago and Illinois Rivers. When it was completed, the canal was the second largest in the world. Now, instead of flowing into Lake Michigan, the Chicago River flowed south into the Illinois River. As a result, Chicago was able to enjoy safer drinking water.

Illinois workplaces became cleaner and safer, too. The huge meatpacking plants in Chicago were very unclean. As a result, the meat sometimes made people who ate it sick. In 1906, Upton Sinclair wrote about life in a meatpacking plant in the novel *The Jungle*. He showed the world just how awful conditions in these plants were.

The Sanitary and Ship Canal opened in 1900, changing the flow of the Chicago River. To this day, the river is said to flow "backward." Chicago's 45 movable bridges (left) let tall ships pass under and down the river.

35

Sinclair became known as a muckraker, which is a writer who wants to expose corruption or unclean conditions. *The Jungle* created public alarm about the way meat was prepared at the plants. As a result, Congress passed laws that forbade unsafe and unclean food packaging.

Another effort to change society for the better did not work out as well. In 1919, the Eighteenth Amendment to the Constitution outlawed the manufacture and sale of alcohol. The new law was called Prohibition. People did not stop buying alcohol. Instead, they depended on criminals to supply it. Criminals formed gangs and used violence to protect their illegal business. Chicago became famous for gangsters who boldly broke the law. One of the most famous gangsters was Al Capone. In 3 years in Chicago, 360 people lost their lives in gang violence. Al Capone was finally convicted and sent to federal prison in 1932. Prohibition ended in 1933, with the Twenty-first Amendment to the U.S. Constitution.

*Al Capone (above) was also known as "Scarface," because his left cheek had a scar from a fight. He was finally convicted in 1931, for trying to avoid paying his income taxes.*

## THE GREAT DEPRESSION

By 1933, Illinois and the rest of the nation were deep in the Great Depression. The Depression was one of the worst crises in the nation's history. It lasted from 1929 until about 1940. Businesses failed and banks closed. Millions of people lost their jobs and life savings. In Illinois alone, 1.5 million people lost their jobs. Coal mines shut down, and half of Illinois miners were out of work. The Illinois Central Railroad fired 30,000 employees because people stopped using the railroad. Without the railroad, farmers were unable to sell their crops. In cities and on farms, many Illinoisans fell into **poverty.**

*Bread lines such as this one in Chicago in 1931 were not uncommon sights during the Great Depression. Many people lost their life savings during the Depression. In Illinois, about 1.5 million people lost their jobs. Soup kitchens in cities helped provide food for the poor.*

President Franklin Roosevelt tried to provide relief from the hardships of the Great Depression. He called his plan the New Deal. Roosevelt changed the way banks operated. The savings of common people would now be protected. He created new programs to put people back to work. In 1933, Roosevelt formed the Civilian Conser-vation Corps (CCC). The Corps worked to beautify state parks and other places. The Works Progress Administration (WPA) was formed in 1935. It built new parks, roads, and bridges. There were also artists who created beautiful **murals** in public schools and post offices.

*Civilian Conservation Corps workers built the lodge (below) at Starved Rock State Park.*

## WORLD WAR II

Illinois and the nation recov-ered from the Great Depres-sion slowly. Another crisis came in 1941. The United States entered World War II (1939–1945) that year. Almost one million Illinois men and women joined the armed ser-vices. About 24,000 of these lost their lives in the war.

# Helping the War Effort

Illinois civilians pitched in to help their country during World War II (1939–1945). Crops from Illinois farms fed soldiers and sailors. To produce more vegetables, more than one million people started gardens called Victory Gardens. They sprouted on empty lots, along railroad tracks, and even on rooftops. People also recycled scrap metal that could be used to make ammunition. The people of Peoria collected a huge pile of aluminum they named Mount Aluminum.

Illinois farms and factories worked overtime to support the war effort. The Pullman Company switched from making railroad cars to building tanks. The International Harvester Company stopped making farm equipment and made gun **carriages.** The Elgin Watch Company made bomb fuses. Plants in Moline, Savanna, Crab Orchard, and Kankakee supplied weapons.

Scientists in Illinois worked on a top-secret war project. They hoped to create the world's first atomic bomb. This would be the most powerful bomb ever made. Experiments that helped make the bomb possible were conducted by scientist Enrico Fermi. Fermi worked in a laboratory beneath the football grandstand at the University of Chicago. Very few people knew about his experiments, but they were important to the war effort. In 1945, the U.S. dropped an atomic bomb on each of the Japanese cities of Hiroshima and Nagasaki. The destruction was horrible, but the event helped to end the war.

*Many women worked in factories making weapons for World War II. These three women (below) are working on aerial torpedoes in 1943, at the International Harvester Company plant in Chicago.*

## THE POSTWAR ERA

During World War II (1939–1945), Illinois colleges provided training for people entering the armed services. After the war, the U.S. government helped pay for college education for **veterans.** Thousands of soldiers returned to Illinois and enrolled. Many new colleges and universities were formed after the war. Some were created by the State of Illinois.

**Suburbs** grew quickly as veterans bought houses. Cars became easier to afford, and people could move from cities and have more space. Suburbs also offered new schools for children.

*Enrico Fermi's (above) research at the University of Chicago helped make the atomic bomb possible. The element fermium was named in his honor.*

After World War II, Illinois became an even more important transportation center. In 1946, O'Hare Airport

## Illinois's Golden Arches

In 1955, a new restaurant called McDonald's opened in Des Plaines, Illinois (left). Before long, there would be thousands of McDonald's restaurants all over the world. They were the idea of a salesman from Oak Park named Ray Kroc. He went into business with the McDonald brothers of San Bernardino, California. Today, McDonald's headquarters are in Oak Brook, Illinois. The company operates a school called Hamburger University, where McDonald's managers receive training.

*O'Hare Airport (above) was named for a World War II U.S. Naval pilot named Edward "Butch" O'Hare. O'Hare won a **Congressional Medal of Honor** for his bravery during the war.*

opened in Chicago. The airport soon became one of the world's busiest. In 1959, the St. Lawrence Seaway opened (see map on page 18). This was a water route that ran from the Great Lakes to the Atlantic Ocean. It allowed large, ocean-going ships to sail to Illinois, which helped the economy.

Farm production in Illinois grew after the war. New technology and machinery made it possible to grow more and work more land. However, only large farms made enough money to pay for the machinery and technology. Many small farmers went out of business, and remaining farms became even larger.

Soybeans were introduced to the United States from Asia in the 1930s. Champaign County became the leading producer of soybeans in the country. Today, Illinois farmers grow about 354 million bushels (12.5 billion liters) of soybeans each year. Of course, corn remains an important crop in Illinois. In fact, McLean County is the top corn-producing county in the nation.

*Today, soybeans (right) are an important crop in Illinois. They have become a popular part of people's diets. Soybeans are used in tofu, and soybean oil is used to make ink, soap, and other products.*

# A Century Closes

In the second half of the twentieth century, Illinoisans were still fighting for equal rights for all. In the 1960s, Illinois Senator Everett Dirksen helped pass national laws that secured rights for minorities. In 1966, Martin Luther King Jr. led protests against unfair housing rules for African Americans in Chicago. King was a leader in the effort to secure civil rights for minorities in the South. To show that injustice existed in the North, too, he came to Chicago. African Americans in Chicago and other cities were denied the chance to live in some all-white neighborhoods. King marched with supporters into all-white neighborhoods to protest this injustice. His marches angered some residents and led to violence.

*Everett Dirksen (below) helped pass the Civil Rights Act of 1964.*

## VIOLENCE IN THE CITIES

In April 1968, Martin Luther King Jr. was murdered in Memphis, Tennessee. **Riots** broke out in Chicago. Nine people died and about five hundred were injured. Rioting also occurred in Carbondale, Alton, and East St. Louis. Because of this violence, many people moved away from cities. By 1970, more Americans lived in **suburbs** than in cities.

*The 1968 Democratic Convention took place August 26–29. Outside the convention, thousands of anti-war protestors clashed with over 11,000 Chicago police (right), as well as Army troops, National Guardsmen, and Secret Service.*

People also protested United States involvement in the Vietnam War. The Vietnam War lasted from 1957 to 1975, but most of the fighting involving U.S. troops took place from 1965 to 1969. During the Democratic National Convention of 1968, thousands of people filled the streets of downtown Chicago to protest the war. In front of television cameras, police and protesters fought on the streets of Chicago. A national television audience watched the violence in shock.

*Ronald Reagan (below) grew up in Dixon, Illinois. Today, visitors can walk through his boyhood home in Dixon.*

## A NEW CONSTITUTION

In the late 1960s, Illinoisans decided it was time for a new state constitution. The existing constitution had been passed in 1870. People believed a more up-to-date document was needed. The new constitution of 1970 aimed to protect the rights of all people. It gives women equal rights and forbids discrimination against those with disabilities.

In 1976, voters elected James Thompson governor. He was reelected three more times, making him the first Illinois governor to serve four terms. In 1980, Illinois native Ronald Reagan was elected president of the United States. Reagan was born in Tampico, Illinois, and grew up in Dixon, Illinois. He served two terms as president.

# Big Suburbs

Some of Illinois's largest cities are **suburbs.** Chicago and Rockford top the list of Illinois's largest cities. After Chicago and Rockford come two Chicago suburbs. Aurora is home to about 143,000 people. It is the third largest city in Illinois. Naperville's population is 128,000, which makes it the fourth largest.

Illinois's population decreased while Thompson and Reagan were in office. In 1950, Illinois was the third most populous state in the nation. By 1980, it was sixth. Illinois lost people and jobs to growing states in the South and Southwest. In the 1980s, crop prices fell and the value of farmland dropped. Some Illinois farmers had no choice but to sell their land and pay debts.

Illinois **industries** went through hard times, too. Many factories closed and workers lost their jobs. However, manufacturers remained among the state's top employers. The state also worked to encourage the growth of other kinds of businesses. Tourism in Galena, Springfield, Chicago, and other cities provided jobs in hotels, restaurants, and other businesses. New industries devoted to providing computer and other high-technology services provided more jobs. The printing and publishing industry is another one of the state's top employers.

## THE TWENTY-FIRST CENTURY

At the start of the twenty-first century, Illinois remained a transportation center. As more and more people traveled by air, Illinois looked for ways to handle increased air traffic.

*James R. Thompson (below) served as governor of Illinois for fourteen years, from 1977 to 1991.*

## The Thompson Center

To honor James Thompson, Illinois named one of its biggest government buildings after him. The James R. Thompson Center (right) in Chicago is home to many state offices.

The state's population continued to grow, as well. In 2000, more than 12 million people lived in Illinois. That is about 1 million more than in 1990. For the first time in 50 years, the population of Chicago grew, too.

*Since 1975, volunteers have been working to restore the land around Fermilab (below) to the native tallgrass prairie that was once there.*

At the same time, Illinoisans worked to protect their environment. In the 1990s, cleanup efforts greatly improved the health of Illinois's rivers. This gave new hope to endangered river species like the river otter. Illinoisans also replanted and restored pieces of the tallgrass **prairie** that once covered the state.

For thousands of years, the rivers and prairies sustained the people who lived in the area. Today, Illinoisans are working to give new life back to the environment. With their efforts, the people and environment of Illinois will continue to flourish well into the future.

# Timeline

| | |
|---|---|
| ca.15,000 B.C.E. | Paleo-Indians migrate into Illinois. |
| 8000 B.C.E. | People of the **Archaic Period** begin planting crops. |
| C.E. 700 | People of the Mississippian Culture build large towns and construct temple mounds. |
| 1655 | Illinois tribes clash with invading Iroquois. |
| 1673 | Louis Jolliet and Jacques Marquette are the first white men to enter Illinois. |
| 1703 | French **missionaries** found the town of Kaskaskia. |
| 1776 | The Declaration of Independence is signed. |
| 1778 | George Rogers Clark's troops capture Cahokia and Kaskaskia during the Revolutionary War (1775–1783). |
| 1783 | The Revolutionary War ends. |
| 1787 | The U.S. Congress makes Illinois part of the Northwest **Territory.** |
| 1803 | **Fort** Dearborn is built at the site of present-day Chicago. |
| 1809 | The U.S. Congress makes Illinois a territory. |
| 1818 | Illinois becomes the twenty-first state on December 3. Kaskaskia becomes its first capital. |
| 1820 | Vandalia becomes the capital of Illinois. |
| 1832 | Illinois settlers defeat the Sauk and Fox tribes during the Black Hawk War. |
| 1836 | Illinois builds the Illinois and Michigan Canal. |
| 1840 | Springfield becomes the capital of Illinois. |
| 1858 | Abraham Lincoln and Stephen A. Douglas debate during their campaign for the U.S. Senate. |
| 1860 | Abraham Lincoln is elected president of the United States. |
| 1861 | The Civil War (1861–1865) begins. |
| 1871 | The Chicago Fire destroys much of Chicago. |
| 1900 | The Chicago Sanitary and Ship Canal is completed. |
| 1913 | Illinois grants women the right to vote in city and presidential elections. |
| 1929 | The Great Depression begins with the crash of the stock market. |
| 1945 | World War II (1939–1945) ends and the United Nations is formed. |
| 1964 | The United States passes civil rights laws. |
| 1968 | The murder of Martin Luther King Jr. sets off **riots** in Chicago and other cities. |
| 1970 | Illinois voters approve a new state constitution. |
| 1980 | Native Illinoisan Ronald Reagan is elected president of the United States. |
| 1986 | James Thompson becomes the first Illinois governor to be elected four times. |
| 1991 | The United States launches a war against Iraq. |
| 2000 | Census shows that Chicago's population grew for the first time in 50 years. |

# Glossary

**abolitionist** person calling for an end to slavery

**archaeologist** person who studies the remains of past human life and activities

**Archaic Period** ca. 8000 B.C.E. to 1000 B.C.E. This is also sometimes broken up into the Early, Middle, and Late Archaic Periods, and dates sometimes differ among sources.

**architect** person who designs buildings and gives advice on their construction

**baptize** purify or cleanse spiritually; baptism is a Christian ritual that uses water and receives a person into the Christian community

**Bering Strait** section of water that separates the continents of Asia and North America at their closest points. When Paleo-Indians first migrated to North America, the water level was lower, exposing a land bridge at this location.

**bison** also sometimes called a buffalo; large, shaggy-maned mammal with short horns and a hump. Bison were once plentiful in North America and were important to the native peoples for food, clothing, and shelter.

**bituminous coal** softer kind of coal that is dug from the ground and burned for fuel. Bituminous coal contains more carbon than some other types and has a high heating value.

**blacksmith** person who makes iron objects by heating them and hammering them on an anvil. Blacksmiths often make horseshoes.

**carriage** movable or fixed support for a gun

**Catholic** of the Roman Catholic faith, which is the Christian church governed by the pope in Rome

**Christianity** religion that came from Jesus Christ and is based on the Bible; Eastern, Roman Catholic, and Protestant churches are Christian

**confederacy** two or more groups that pledge to act together, especially for defense against attack

**Congressional Medal of Honor** military decoration awarded by the U.S. Congress for exceptional bravery at the risk of life in combat with an enemy

**crude** rough; not carefully made

**extinct** no longer living

**fault** fracture in the earth's crust

**fort** strong building used for defense against enemy attack

**French and Indian War** war that took place in America from 1754 to 1763, between the French and their Native American friends on one side, and the British and their Native American friends on the other

**grange** national organization that works to help farmers

**Ice Age** period of time when a large part of the earth was covered with glaciers and the temperatures were cooler

**immigrant** person who comes into a foreign country to make a new home

**inauguration** public and formal ceremony of placing a person in office

**industry** kind of business

**malaria** disease caused by mosquito bites resulting in fever and chills

**mastodon** large, extinct animal, similar to an elephant, with tusks and shaggy hair

**mission** place where missionaries live and work; a missionary is a person sent by a church to spread its religion

**mural** large picture that is painted or put on a wall

**Nobel Peace Prize** yearly prize given to those who work for the interests of peace and humanity

**nomad** person who doesn't live in any one location, but moves around to be close to a supply of food

**peat** soft material in the ground formed when grass and plants die

**pelt** skin taken from an animal

**plaza** public square in a city or town

**poverty** condition of being poor

**prairie** large area of flat land with a lot of grass and very few trees

**prehistoric** from the time before history was written

**rebel** soldier who fought for the Confederacy (Southern states in rebellion) in the Civil War

**riot** great disorder, confusion, or violence by a crowd of people; to take part in a riot

**sacred ritual** important and honored form or system of actions, especially in a religion

**skyscraper** very tall building

**Stone Age** first known time in which people used stone tools; of this time

**stronghold** fort or other place controlled by a group of people

**suburb** city or town just outside a larger city

**tenement** old, crowded apartment in the poor part of a city

**territory** area of land in the United States that is not organized as a state, but has its own local government

**Underground Railroad** system in the United States in which people who were against slavery secretly helped escaped slaves reach the North or Canada

**veteran** person who has served in the armed forces during a war

**wigwam** dome-shaped Native American hut with a frame of poles covered with bark, rush mats, or animal hides

**woolly mammoth** large, extinct animal, similar to an elephant, with shaggy hair and long tusks that curve upward

# More Books to Read

Anderson, Kathy P. *Illinois.* Minneapolis, Minn.: Lerner Publishing, 2001.

Bial, Raymond. *Where Lincoln Walked.* New York: Walker and Company, 1998.

Kay, Betty Carlson. *Illinois From A to Z.* Champaign, Ill.: University of Illinois Press, 2000.

Marsh, Carole. *Illinois Jeopardy.* Peachtree City, Ga.: Gallopade International, 2000.

Marsh, Carole. *My First Book about Illinois.* Peachtree City, Ga.: Gallopade International, 2000.

## Fiction:

Peck, Richard. *A Long Way from Chicago.* New York: Penguin Putnam, 1998.

Peck, Richard. *A Year down Yonder.* New York: Penguin Putnam, 2000.

# Index

# About the Author

Andrew Santella lives in Trout Valley, Illinois, and is a lifelong resident of the state of Illinois. He is the author of 25 nonfiction books for children. He also writes for publications such as *GQ* and the *New York Times Book Review*.